CELEBRATING THE CITY OF MILAN

Celebrating the City of Milan

Walter the Educator

Silent King Books

SILENT KING BOOKS

SKB

Copyright © 2024 by Walter the Educator

All rights reserved. No part of this book may be reproduced in any manner whatsoever without written permission except in the case of brief quotations embodied in critical articles and reviews.

First Printing, 2024

Disclaimer
This book is a literary work; the story is not about specific persons, locations, situations, and/or circumstances unless mentioned in a historical context. Any resemblance to real persons, locations, situations, and/or circumstances is coincidental. This book is for entertainment and informational purposes only. The author and publisher offer this information without warranties expressed or implied. No matter the grounds, neither the author nor the publisher will be accountable for any losses, injuries, or other damages caused by the reader's use of this book. The use of this book acknowledges an understanding and acceptance of this disclaimer.

Celebrating the City of Milan is a collectible souvenir book that belongs to the Celebrating Cities Book Series by Walter the Educator. Collect them all and more books at WaltertheEducator.com

MILAN

In the heart of Lombardy, where histories conspire,

Celebrating the City of

Milan

A city woven with threads of time, rich with fire.

Celebrating the City of
Milan

Milan, a jewel set in the northern crown,

Celebrating the City of

Milan

Where ancient whispers meet the modern town.

Celebrating the City of

Milan

Beneath a sky that blushes at dawn's kiss,

Celebrating the City of

Milan

The streets of Milan hum with a bustling bliss.

Celebrating the City of

Milan

Gothic spires of the Duomo stretch towards the sky,

Celebrating the City of
Milan

Where saints in marble repose, dream, and sigh.

Celebrating the City of

Milan

Each stone a story, each corner a verse,

Celebrating the City of

Milan

A symphony of life in Milan's diverse purse.

Celebrating the City of

Milan

From Leonardo's strokes to the fashion elite,

The spirit of creation finds its heartbeat.

Celebrating the City of Milan

Brera's art beckons with colors so grand,

Celebrating the City of
Milan

A gallery where brush and canvas command.

Celebrating the City of
Milan

The echoes of masters, both old and new,

Celebrating the City of
Milan

In every stroke, in every hue.

Celebrating the City of

Milan

Navigli's canals mirror the twilight's glow,

Celebrating the City of Milan

Where lovers and poets drift and flow.

Celebrating the City of

Milan

The water's whisper, a serenade sweet,

Celebrating the City of

Milan

To the cobblestones that cradle our feet.

Celebrating the City of

Milan

La Scala's stage, where operatic dreams ignite,

Celebrating the City of

Milan

Aria's crescendo pierces the night.

Celebrating the City of

Milan

In velvet seats, hearts swell and soar,

Celebrating the City of Milan

To music that weaves through Milan's core.

Celebrating the City of
Milan

Sforza's castle stands, a sentinel bold,

Celebrating the City of Milan

Guarding secrets of stories untold.

Celebrating the City of

Milan

Within its walls, the past comes alive,

Celebrating the City of

Milan

Whispering of times when knights did thrive.

Celebrating the City of

Milan

Galleria's arches gleam underfoot,

Celebrating the City of

Milan

A mosaic of commerce, of elegance soot.

Celebrating the City of

Milan

Fashion's pulse, in threads so fine,

Celebrating the City of Milan

Defines the vogue, the elegant line.

Celebrating the City of

Milan

The legacy of Milan, carved in stone,

Celebrating the City of

Milan

A reminder of dreams, now fully grown.

Celebrating the City of

Milan

In every corner, in every face,

Celebrating the City of

Milan

The story of Milan, a timeless embrace.

Celebrating the City of Milan

Thus, we celebrate this city so grand,

Celebrating the City of Milan

With a poem that pays homage to this land.

Celebrating the City of

Milan

Milan, where dreams are woven in gold,

Celebrating the City of

Milan

Tales, forever bold.

Celebrating the City of

Milan

ABOUT THE CREATOR

Walter the Educator is one of the pseudonyms for Walter Anderson. Formally educated in Chemistry, Business, and Education, he is an educator, an author, a diverse entrepreneur, and he is the son of a disabled war veteran. "Walter the Educator" shares his time between educating and creating. He holds interests and owns several creative projects that entertain, enlighten, enhance, and educate, hoping to inspire and motivate you.

Follow, find new works, and stay up to date
with Walter the Educator™
at WaltertheEducator.com

Milton Keynes UK
Ingram Content Group UK Ltd.
UKHW020742110724
445512UK00011B/264